Original title:
Sands of Dreams

Copyright © 2025 Creative Arts Management OÜ
All rights reserved.

Author: Theodore Sinclair
ISBN HARDBACK: 978-1-80581-627-0
ISBN PAPERBACK: 978-1-80581-154-1
ISBN EBOOK: 978-1-80581-627-0

Deserted Fantasies

In a land where wishes stew,
I found a dancing kangaroo.
He wore a hat, a silly sight,
And juggled pillows, what a fright!

With llamas planning a ballet,
They twirled and spun in bright array.
But every time the music played,
They lost their steps and got dismayed.

Glistening Horizons

There's a beach made of bubblegum,
Where seagulls strut and start to hum.
A crab in shades, he moves with flair,
While fish compete in stylish air!

A dolphin flips with sheer delight,
Showing off his moves so tight.
He shouts, "Come watch my surfboard skills!"
But falls flat into a wave of frills.

Tides of Imagination

A pirate ships on maple syrup,
He sails through clouds like a hiccup.
His crew, a band of twinkling stars,
They toast with mugs of chocolate bars!

Onward to find that treasure chest,
Filled with candy and a funny jest.
But every map leads to a prank,
Like finding socks in the ocean's bank!

Fragments of the Infinite

In a world of colorful cheese,
Where mice wear boots and dance with ease.
They twirl around on pizza crust,
And giggle loudly, so they must!

With each bite taken, laughter peeks,
As melted moments slide on peaks.
In every crumb, a story spun,
Of silly lands where joy's the sun.

Lost in the Grit

In a pile of flour, I tried to bake,
But ended up with an odd pancake.
My spatula flew, took a dip in the mix,
Now my breakfast is stuck in a fix.

I wore flip-flops to a sandstorm's show,
My toes got buried, it's a silly row.
The sun was shining, it looked so neat,
But my hat took flight, now it's scared of defeat.

Beneath the Surface

I jumped in puddles, thought I'd find gold,
Instead, I found a frog, quite bold.
He croaked a tune, and danced with flair,
Now we're the stars of a swampy affair.

My snorkel's stuck, I'm upside down,
Fish are giggling at this old clown.
They've seen it all, my wild, flailing kicks,
At least my goggles still look like slick tricks.

Fading Illusions

My ice cream cone slid out of my hand,
A drip, a plop—oh, isn't life grand?
I chased the drips as they melted away,
What a sticky mess to brighten my day!

I tried to catch whispers on a soft breeze,
Caught a fly instead, I'm hoping it flees.
With nets made of dreams and hopes in the air,
I might as well just give laughter a share.

Chasing Fleeting Moments

A piñata burst, all candy takes flight,
I swung too hard and dark turned to light.
A lollipop hit me, oh how it stuck,
Spinning in circles, I guess I'm out of luck!

I set out to catch a bright, falling star,
But tripped on my laces; my feet went too far.
A tumble, a laugh, I'm the star of the night,
Mischief and giggles, oh what a sight!

Dreamcatcher's Lament

My net caught a fish, oh what a sight,
But it swam away, giving me a fright.
I dreamt of a feast, all glitter and glee,
But it turns out my dreams just like to flee.

With visions of cupcakes, so fluffy and round,
Yet I woke up to find crumbs scattered around.
My catch of the day is now just a joke,
A feast for my mind, but my belly bespoke.

Labyrinth of Hopes

I wandered through hopes like a lost little cat,
Chasing my tail, but where is it at?
Every corner I turn, confusion and cheer,
My dreams are a maze, not so crystal clear.

I found a fine cheese, it smelled like delight,
But it turned to a dream, hidden from sight.
I laughed at my quest, it's a comedy show,
In a maze of my hopes, the only way is go slow.

Veil of Enchantment

Behind silken curtains, a circus unfolds,
With clowns riding bikes and performing bold.
A hat full of rabbits, they giggle and pop,
As I reach for the magic, they all start to hop.

The wands are just sticks, and the spells are like cheese,
With laughter and giggles, I float on the breeze.
The trick is quite simple, just don't take a poke,
For behind every dream is a hilarious joke.

Timeless Tread

I've danced through the ages, so light on my feet,
With time as my partner, it's quite the treat.
We whirl and we twirl, through decades of fun,
But I trip on my shoelace, oh where has it run?

The clock ticks away, but I'm stuck in a spin,
With sneakers of laughter, I can't help but grin.
Chronicles of giggles, moments to spread,
In this timeless waltz, I embrace what I dread.

Mirage of Tomorrow

In a desert of wishes, I trip on a whim,
A cactus with glasses, his vision is dim.
The sun plays hide and seek with my hat,
While camels in tuxedos dance like a cat.

Each grain tells a joke that tickles my toes,
But I laugh so hard, I forget how it goes.
With sunburned laughter, I float like a mote,
Chasing shadows that giggle, I dream and I gloat.

Dunes of Desire

A beach ball with sunglasses rolls past with a grin,
It says, 'Chase your dreams, but don't let them win!'
The seagulls are gossiping, squawking with flair,
While I build my ambitions with sand in my hair.

I saw a sandcastle throw a wild dance,
With windows of candy, it took a small chance.
The tide told a story of plans gone awry,
As I dodge all the waves that bubble and sigh.

Twilight Reveries

Under a sky painted in ice cream delight,
I sip on my dreams, oh what a sweet sight!
A llama in pajamas sings softly to me,
As stars waltz around like they've lost the marquee.

Fireflies chuckle as they scribble in light,
Drawing noodles and mountains in the velvety night.
With giggles and grins, we caper and sway,
Ignoring the mundane as we tumble and play.

Footprints in the Mist

Waking up silly, I tumble from bed,
With dreams on my shirt, and a hat on my head.
The fog is a blanket that plays peek-a-boo,
While rabbits with top hats perform their debut.

Each step that I take leaves a riddle to solve,
As I march through this world where the weird evolves.
With every soft squish, I giggle and muse,
At a path paved with puddles of laughter-infused.

Gilded Fantasies in the Dunes

In a land where camels dance and prance,
A mirage winks, inviting a chance.
Juggling dates, oh what a sight,
Sandcastles rise under the moonlight.

Tumbleweeds roll like they're in a race,
While lizards play tag in this sunlit space.
Flip-flops flapping, laughter erupts,
As we sip sweet tea from golden cups.

The Oasis of Hopes

In the middle of nowhere, a fountain appears,
With ducks in sombreros, we laugh through our tears.
Watermelon slices, so juicy and bright,
A picnic of giggles, pure delight!

A palm tree that winks, wearing shades just right,
While sunbathers toast under the daytime light.
Tanning our dreams on this funny terrain,
In an oasis where joy cannot be contained.

Breath of the Desert Night

The stars hold a concert, a laugh and a cheer,
As coyotes croon tunes that only we hear.
Under the cover of a blanket so wide,
We dance with the shadows, full of desert pride.

Glow-in-the-dark cacti sway to the beat,
While tumbleweeds twist in a rhythm so sweet.
The cool desert whispers, dreams take their flight,
In the wild of the night, everything feels right.

Mirage of Lost Aspirations

A vision appears, which looks like a gem,
But all that it holds is a sad little hem.
We chase after wishes, like dogs on the run,
Only to find, we forgot how to have fun!

Umbrellas and surfboards in this dusty expanse,
A sand-surfing competition? Oh, take a chance!
We tumble and giggle, as the sun starts to sink,
In this goofy adventure, we finally think!

Reflections in a Dusty Mirage

In a land of twirling dust,
Llamas dance and twirl, oh, what a fuss!
They wear sombreros, flapping wide,
Chasing shadows side by side.

Mirages giggle, take a dip,
While cacti join in silly quips.
A tumbleweed laughs, rolls on by,
To a cactus party, oh my, oh my!

Threads of Time's Gentle Crystal

In crystal caves where giggles dwell,
Time winks and tells a joke or two.
Old clocks skip beats, dance like a spell,
While hourglasses sip morning dew.

The minutes wear polka-dots bright,
And seconds juggle with all their might.
A playful breeze whispers in glee,
As time turns back for a cup of tea!

Whispers of Time

Time tiptoes with gum on its shoe,
Accidentally stepping on dreams anew.
It holds a mirror, makes faces at fate,
While giggling at days that can't wait.

With a wink and a nudge, in a cheeky jest,
It tells the past, 'You've done your best!'
So let's toss our worries, give laughter a try,
And ride on the wings of a cloud passing by!

Shifting Echoes

Echoes dance in a wobbly line,
They wear mismatched shoes, oh so divine.
With a hop and a skip, they skip to the beat,
In this silly place where giggles meet.

Every shout is a tickle, a sparkly tease,
As echoes bounce off the floppy trees.
A chorus of laughter and playful calls,
In shifting shadows, the merriment sprawls!

When the Winds of Longing Sing

When the breeze whispers sweet, like a cat on parade,
I chase after tumbleweeds, in my flip-flop brigade.
Laughing at clouds that tickle my nose,
While dashing for ice cream, oh, where did it go?

The wind plays tricks, like a sneaky old fox,
Stealing my hat and then hiding my socks.
I tumble and giggle, I slip and I sway,
As my giggles float off in a whimsical way.

Secrets Buried in Golden Light

Beneath the sun's playful rays, treasures lie deep,
A sandwich I've hidden, oh, slice it and weep!
With ants in a frenzy, a picnic's delight,
As I lounge in my chair, what a curious sight!

I hide my candy stash in a sun-warmed shoe,
But a squirrel in shades thinks it belongs to him too!
Chasing each other 'round the lemonade stand,
I crown him the king; we both take a stand.

Unraveled Dreams Beneath the Sun

In a hammock that's swaying, I dream of a race,
But I'm tangled in fabric, what a comical place!
I wave at the clouds, they snicker and tease,
As I wriggle and giggle, swaying with ease.

I tried catching butterflies, oh what a blunder,
They laughed at my shoes, those colorful wonders.
With wings made of whispers, they dart and they dive,
While I chase them like puppies, feeling alive!

The Dance of Shimmering Illusions

Once I saw a mirage that danced on the ground,
Waving like a dancer, swaying all around.
I clapped in applause, what a marvelous show,
Only to trip on a rock, oh no, oh no!

Mirrors and bubbles float up in the air,
I chase after giggles, as light as a hair.
Reality winks, and the fun never ends,
As I dance with my shadow, the best of old friends.

Threads of Starlit Visions

A hamster in a space suit,
Orbiting a cheese moon.
He claims to write a novel,
But just hums a silly tune.

With stars made out of candy,
He dances on the beams.
A comet made of marshmallows,
Is the best of all his dreams.

His rocket's powered by laughter,
Fuelled by giggles and cheer.
He's off to find the treasure,
Oh look, it's just a tear!

So if you see him zoom by,
With nuts and bolts in tow.
Wave at that silly astronaut,
And join in on the show!

The Mirage Keeper's Tale

In a desert made of pudding,
A custard castle stands.
The keeper tells a tall tale,
With sprinkles in both hands.

Goldfish swim through giggles,
In fountains of whipped cream.
They splash and laugh in circles,
Living life just like a dream.

A camel wearing glasses,
Reads books under a tree.
He finds the tales quite funny,
About birds that play like bees.

So join the mirage keeper,
With laughter as your guide.
In this sugary oasis,
There's always joy inside!

Labyrinth of Shifting Shadows

In a maze of silly shadows,
Where every corner shines.
A cat in funky pajamas,
Sips tea with cheese and vines.

He laughs at all the mirrors,
That show a goofy face.
"Am I a lion or a puppy?"
He jumps with endless grace.

The walls whisper jokes and riddles,
As the cacti break dance.
A cactus in a tutu,
Invites you for a chance.

So wander through this labyrinth,
With giggles as your map.
You'll never quite feel lost here,
Just fall into a laugh!

Harvest Moon over Dusty Realms

Under the glowing harvest moon,
A scarecrow starts to sing.
He spills corny jokes and laughter,
While roosters do their thing.

Fields of popcorn burst with joy,
The corn stalks sway and sway.
With chipmunks wearing top hats,
They waltz the night away.

A tractor joins the party,
With wheels that dance around.
It twirls with all the critters,
In this night's merry sound.

So raise a glass of apple juice,
To laughter in the night.
In this dusty, cheerful realm,
Everything feels just right!

Tapestry of Forgotten Tomorrows

In a land where wishes bounce,
A jester lost at the pounce.
He juggles clocks with a grin,
While the cat swipes, 'Let the fun begin!'

Frogs in tuxedos leap around,
Chasing dreams that won't be found.
Each hop a giggle—what a sight,
Charmed by stars that feel just right.

The sun thinks it's a giant pie,
Clouds serve slices to the sky.
Oh, how we'd laugh if we could see,
The universe's wild trickery!

So twirl your hopes on this fine day,
Join the folly, don't be gray.
For the fabric that we weave and mend,
Is stitched in humor, that won't end.

Timeless Voices in the Abyss

Echoes giggle in the mist,
Whispering secrets that twist and twist.
Voices calling from afar,
Cracking jokes beneath the star!

Fish with hats swim in debates,
Arguing about dinner plates.
'What's for lunch?'—a whale replies,
'Three courses and a fishy surprise!'

An octopus plays the ukulele,
While a crab performs in ballet.
Such antics in this endless night,
Where laughter twinkles with delight.

So let's dive deep and take a chance,
Join the creatures in their dance.
For in the depths, mischief reigns,
And joy is fished from playful veins.

Serpentine Paths of the Heart

Winding paths like tangled jokes,
Lead us to the land of folks.
Squirrels rapping 'neath the trees,
Playing cards with bumblebees!

A hedgehog writes a love letter,
To a snail, says 'You're much better!'
With tiny hearts they build their dreams,
Oh, the giggles, oh, the schemes!

Lost balloons float past the moon,
Dancing to a silly tune.
Each twist and turn brings a giggle,
As we follow love, we wiggle!

So laugh along this winding way,
Where hearts can rhyme and play all day.
For every corner holds a cheer,
In this playful path, hold dear.

Fragments of Elysian Landscapes

In a field where daisies talk,
Mice parade and squirrels walk.
They trade their cheese for joy and fun,
Under a sky where rainbows run!

With wobbly legs, the rabbits race,
Bumping into each other's face.
Cheering loud for every hare,
While piglets giggle in the air.

A breeze blows sweet with candy cheer,
As butterflies swoop down near.
They tease the flowers, 'What a sight!'
In this world of sheer delight!

So come and twirl in whimsy's hand,
Join the laughter across the land.
For fragments sparkle all around,
In this landscape—joy abounds!

Lullaby of the Dunes

In a land where camels hum,
And the cactus spins a tale,
The tumbleweed starts to strum,
With a dance that will prevail.

The sun is playing hide and seek,
As lizards wear their shades of green,
A sassy mouse begins to squeak,
With a laugh that's quite obscene.

The breeze is telling silly jokes,
While flip-flops gather dust on racks,
Cacti tickle with their pokes,
As waves of sand do silly hacks.

So lie back and enjoy the scene,
Where giggles float like kites in air,
The world here feels like a dream,
With laughter weaving everywhere.

Driftwood of Memory

Old driftwood starts to chat and tease,
With stories of wild beachy days,
It sways and creaks with such a breeze,
While jellyfish show off their ways.

Crabs take selfies with a flair,
As each wave hugs a salty kiss,
The seagulls dance without a care,
In a world that's pure sandy bliss.

The surfboards laugh at worn-out tricks,
Recalling rides from years gone by,
While barnacles click like old flicks,
As the sun waves slowly goodbye.

So gather 'round this wooden sage,
And listen close to tales they weave,
For memories sizzle like a page,
With laughter no one would believe.

Illumination in Silence

In the quiet of a twinkling night,
Where stars play hide-and-seek above,
A firefly dances with delight,
Sending sparkles like a hug.

The sand whispers secrets of the sea,
As crickets strum their musical song,
An octopus joins in with glee,
Pretending it's where it belongs.

The moon grins with a devious smile,
While shadows play at hide and seek,
A cactus winks in perfect style,
And the night air begins to speak.

So revel in this glowing trance,
Where silence shares a joyous scream,
In the cosmos, take a chance,
And ride on waves of idle dream.

Harmonics of the Soul

In the desert, beats a funny tune,
As the rattlesnakes tap their feet,
The sunflowers bop—who knew?
While shadows sway to the heat.

The tumbleweed rolls on to the beat,
As lizards stage a wild charade,
With every wiggle, it can't be beat,
In the sun where fun won't fade.

The wind is mixing sounds of cheer,
While cactus pranks the wandering eye,
They join in laughter loud and clear,
Where humor floats like clouds in sky.

So dance along this joyful stroll,
With laughter whispering, oh so whole,
In this quirky, playful control,
Find the magic in your soul!

Palette of Dreams

In a jar of silly paints,
I mix my shades of joy.
A brush that squeaks and taunts,
Turns blue to a dancing toy.

With every stroke, I chuckle,
As swirls of giggles rise.
A rooster wears a tutu,
In my wild, uncharted skies.

Colors bounce like bunnies,
As pink turns into green.
A masterpiece of laughter,
Made by a goofball's sheen.

In this canvas of nonsense,
The world just can't be bleak.
For every silly scribble,
A smile is what we seek.

Glimmers in Time

Tick-tock on the wall clock,
Winks at me in glee.
It's always half past pudding,
Can you get there with me?

Naps are taken with candy,
While whispers dance on air.
Silly thoughts march in line,
With polka-dots to spare.

Time spills like ice cream,
Across the sunny floor.
We giggle at the moment,
Then we dream and snore.

Every second's a wink,
A jest from the divine.
In this race of mischief,
We're forever out of time.

Chasing Shadows

I chase my shadow's antics,
Across the bright sidewalk.
It giggles in the sunlight,
And spins with every talk.

A shadow's playing tricks,
A hop, a jump, a slide.
Just when I catch it quick,
It's off to play and hide.

Around the corner sneaky,
It sprinkles goofy glee.
We race through leaves and laughter,
A playful shadow spree.

In this dance of silliness,
There's never time to pout.
For every leap and bound,
A chuckle's what it's about.

Tides of the Heart

Waves of giggles crashing,
On shores of silly dreams.
My heart's a beach ball bouncing,
In sunlight's golden beams.

With every splash and giggle,
The tide pulls at my feet.
I dance like a jellyfish,
In rhythm, oh so sweet.

Seaweed tickles my ankles,
While seagulls sing out loud.
They squawk a funny tune,
As I join the sandy crowd.

At twilight, laughter lingers,
And ripples hug the land.
In the ocean's gentle squeeze,
We find joy hand in hand.

Realm of Wisp and Wonder

In a land where giggles grow,
Jellybeans jump to and fro.
Clouds wear hats, and bugs wear ties,
Winking owls drop silly cries.

Bouncing bunnies bake some pies,
Blowing bubbles made of fries.
Dancing lizards sing a tune,
Underneath the laughing moon.

Chasing shadows on a whim,
To the flow of a whimsy hymn.
Snails in slippers slide and race,
In this wacky, wondrous place.

Tickles spread from shelf to shelf,
Tidy mice read tales themselves.
Every corner hides a jest,
In this realm, we laugh the best.

Voyage of the Mind

A ship made of marshmallows bright,
Sails the rivers of delight.
Captain Squeak in a funny hat,
Guides a crew of playful rats.

Whimsical waves of ice cream swirl,
As gummy bears perform a twirl.
Navigate through pudding seas,
With chocolate ducks that make you sneeze.

Pirates with hair of cotton candy,
Dance and sing, all just so dandy.
Treasure maps made of taffy string,
Lead to pots of giggles they bring.

At sunset, the sky's a treat,
As jellyfish jive with shuffling feet.
In this voyage, every smile's free,
In a realm where we laugh with glee.

Kaleidoscope of Fantasies

Through a lens of jelly and jam,
I see the world of a laughing clam.
Colors swirl in a silly dance,
As rainbows twirl in a wobbly prance.

Kites made of pancakes soar high,
With syrup trails that wave goodbye.
Ducks in tuxedos take a dive,
While jellybeans bounce, feeling alive.

Cherries play hopscotch, giggling loud,
As clouds gather in a sugar-shrouded crowd.
Unicorns with polka dot tails,
Share secrets whispered through sugary trails.

In this kaleidoscope bright and bold,
Every giggle is a tale retold.
With whimsy wrapped in each small scene,
Life's a festival, sweet and serene.

Essence of the Eternal

In a land where time takes a break,
And every moment's a piece of cake.
Tick-tock goes a clock made of cheese,
As laughter floats on a gentle breeze.

Worms in bow ties serenade trees,
While daffodils dance with the bees.
A fountain of giggles spews delight,
As fireflies wink in the soft twilight.

Floating through a bubble filled with cheer,
Time stands still, and worries disappear.
Jesters leap from every small nook,
In a never-ending storybook.

With every chuckle sewn in place,
Life's a laughter, a silly race.
In this eternal jest we find,
The sweetness of a playful mind.

Ethereal Reflections

In a puddle that giggles and winks,
A fish wears a hat, or so it thinks.
A cloud races by, with a wink and a grin,
Dropping jokes on the waves, where the fun begins.

A mirror of laughter, wrapped in delight,
The moon spills its secrets under starlight.
Floating on dreams that chase after glee,
While turtles play cards with a friendly bee.

A smile in the breeze, a tickle in time,
Where whispers of silliness dance in sublime.
The world laughs along, a merry parade,
And the night wears a crown, just like a charade.

So we giggle while pondering, hearts in the sky,
Counting silly wishes that drift and fly.
In every reflection, a chuckle we find,
In this whimsical realm, where nonsense is kind.

Breeze of Desires

A breeze rolled in, with a mischievous grin,
It tangled the hair of a dandelion twin.
They danced to a tune of 'What if and why',
And made nonchalant promises with a sigh.

A rubber duck party, where bubbles explode,
Riding on waves of a foamy abode.
Requests for more laughs and infinite cheer,
As gulls swap their stories with the wind in their ear.

From sunbeams that skip to the moon's playful tease,
Every tickle and twist sets the heart at ease.
So let's catch the laughter that flutters so free,
Like kites in the sky, the happiest spree.

The wishes we whisper, as light as a sigh,
Drift with the swirls of the clouds wandering by.
With each gust of whimsy, our spirits arise,
In this breezy domain where each giggle flies.

Spirit of the Mirage

In a desert of dreams, where shadows prance,
A cactus wears shades, ready to dance.
It twirls and it sways, with legs made of sand,
While visions of llamas lend a helping hand.

Laughing coyotes perform a wild show,
Telling tall tales of the moon's brilliant glow.
They spin on their tails while the stars clap along,
Joining in jest with a jubilant song.

An oasis of chuckles, where water is sweet,
And every refreshing sip brings laughter's heartbeat.
Jumping jacks play with the mirage's delight,
Chasing their giggles until day meets the night.

So, follow the shimmer where laughter resides,
In a land made of whimsy, where fun is our guide.
Every twist of the fate, every quirky charade,
In this spirit of laughter, all worries will fade.

Translucent Currents

Underneath the waves, where the jellyfish groove,
Fish wear tuxedos, showing off their moves.
They form a conga line when the ship passes by,
With octopuses clapping for a sea-bound high-fly.

The shells hold their breath, as the currents all smile,
Whispering secrets with a whimsical style.
They paint the water with giggles and glee,
Where turtles compete in a slow-motion spree.

In the tides of delight, where laughter is found,
A sea of confetti swirls all around.
The seaweed's a dancer, swaying with flair,
In a balletic twist, floating light as air.

So sail on the ripples, embrace the fun ride,
With creatures of mirth always close by our side.
For in these translucent currents we roam,
The laughter we capture becomes our true home.

Pathways of Whimsy

In a land where socks do roam,
They dance and sing but not at home.
With mismatched shoes on every foot,
They chuckle loud beneath a fruit.

Cactus hats and jelly beans,
A world of laughter, silly scenes.
With giggles floating in the air,
Even the chairs begin to swear.

The sun wears shades of purple hue,
While kangaroos sip morning dew.
They leap with joy, they hop and twirl,
In this strange, upside-down world.

So take a step on paths of fun,
There's less to worry, more to run.
Embrace the quirks, don't hesitate,
For whimsy rules, so celebrate!

Fragrance of the Ether

In the kitchen, a smell so grand,
Berries jammed in a big, round hand.
Spilling giggles, frosting spry,
Spoons take flight, oh my, oh my!

A whiff of taffy in the breeze,
Lollipops hang from trendy trees.
The scent of laughter fills the air,
With sprinkles dancing without a care.

A pickle dressed in polka dots,
Winks at cheese from kitchen pots.
They throw a bash with toast and jelly,
While cupcakes whirl on jelly-belly.

So float on scents of fun today,
With pastry dreams that dance and sway.
In every bite, a world delight,
With flavors bold and hearts so light!

Symphony of Illusions

A trumpet made of candy cane,
Blows a tune that melts the rain.
Beasts in tuxedos, quite a sight,
Twirl and skip into the night.

A chorus of ducks in tuxedo ties,
Chanting truths and goofy lies.
Invisible violins play along,
As they all sing a silly song.

A bear in boots rides on a bike,
Sailing through the air, what a hike!
The laughter echoes through the trees,
While squirrels juggle with such ease.

So close your eyes, let's make a wish,
For wacky tunes and jazz so swish.
In this grand show of whimsy bright,
Every note will spark delight!

Footfalls of the Spirit

Footprints shimmer on the ground,
Leading where the giggles sound.
A ghost in socks does shimmy well,
With ticklish toes that break the spell.

A dance-off with a floppy hat,
Then spins and twirls, where's the cat?
He's twirling too, with a little bow,
While shadows grin, and stars say wow!

A specter serenades the moon,
With hiccups bursting like a balloon.
The night chuckles and moonbeams play,
In an orchestra of light and fray.

So join the spirit, take a chance,
For every stumble is a dance.
With footfalls echoing in the night,
The world's a dream, a merry flight!

Whirlwind of Whispers

In the corner, a sock waves,
It dances like it found a rave.
A broom joins in, all swept away,
While the cat just yawns, 'What a play!'

A teacup chats with a dusty book,
It shares secrets from every nook.
Laughter spills, like tea unchaste,
What a show; let's not waste!

The clock tick-tocks in a silly jig,
It's late, but who cares? Let's dig!
A spoon winks at a fork with flair,
Together, they form a lively pair!

In the pantry, a pickle prances,
With marshmallows, they take their chances.
Jellybeans hop on the kitchen floor,
Saying, "Join us! There's always more!"

Essence of Ephemerality

A bubble floats, its journey brief,
It pops with joy, 'Oh, what a relief!'
A gnome grins wide beside the sink,
Surprising everyone with a wink.

Silly socks play hide-and-seek,
Under the bed, they giggle and squeak.
While a moth flirts with the lamp's warm glow,
'Oops!' It says, 'I'll just go slow!'

A rubber chicken struts with pride,
Chasing the dog, who runs to hide.
The goldfish laughs, as fish do best,
"Thank goodness I'm in my watery nest!"

In the garden, weeds throw a ball,
While roses tease with their petals tall.
They tumble and laugh in the sunny light,
Who knew gardening could be such a sight?

Whims of the Hand

Paper airplanes fly with a cheer,
But crash into pillows—never fear!
A pencil dreams of being a sword,
In a battle where notes are scored.

Sticky tape weaves a wild tale,
As it wraps around an old snail.
Markers race to find their place,
On a canvas of splashes; what a space!

Folders gossip of lost pages,
While rulers share their ancient sages.
Scissors snip with a playful dance,
Crafting chaos that dares to prance!

In the chaos, a glue stick sings,
Of friendships and all the joy it brings.
With laughter, they create their own show,
In a world where everything can glow!

Threads of the Past

A dusty quilt hums a lullaby,
It whispers stories as moths drift by.
Old buttons jingle like tiny bells,
Echoing secrets of time they tell.

A rocking chair creaks, it's quite the sage,
Swaying gently, it turns the page.
While cobwebs dance in the evening light,
Showing off their craft in the twilight.

Photos giggle in their frames so bright,
With smiles that linger in soft moonlight.
A doorknob spins, inviting the breeze,
Replaying memories like a teasing tease!

In the attic, an old trunk snores,
Filled with laughter and forgotten chores.
With each open flap, a world takes flight,
Turning echoes into pure delight!

Flickering Lanterns

In a world where shadows dance,
Lanterns flicker with a chance.
A cat wearing a tiny hat,
Prances by a sleeping rat.

The moonbeam tries to steal a kiss,
While frogs jump around in bliss.
A talking tree sings out of tune,
And shoes chase after a wayward balloon.

Goblins cheat at hopscotch games,
While trolls hurl pie and laugh with names.
A jester juggles colored beans,
As fairies bake bizarre machines.

In this place where whimsy reigns,
Every chuckle breaks the chains.
So grab a friend and tag along,
In a world where the funny belongs.

Behind the Veil

Behind the curtain, laughter swells,
A dragon sneezes, rings like bells.
With mismatched shoes and polka dots,
The wizard trips and tumbles, blots!

The fairy peeks, with a wink so sly,
While gnomes shoot glitter in the sky.
A pickle sings a happy tune,
As mice dance under the light of the moon.

A puppet with a wobbly knee,
Tells jokes about a bumblebee.
The crowd erupts in cheerful squeals,
As magic pies spin on wheels.

So lift the veil and join the fun,
In a world where mischief's never done.
It's a circus with charm and cheer,
And every giggle brings us near.

Gaze of Infinity

With wide eyes, we peek within,
A circus where the chaos spins.
The candy clouds float on by,
While squirrels wear caps and sigh.

Balloons escape, they float so high,
A fish in a top hat waves goodbye.
The sun's a lazy, grinning face,
Chasing shadows all over the place.

A jellybean plays hopscotch right,
While donuts dance in the pale moonlight.
With each step, the giggles grow,
As we dance through this wondrous show.

So let us twirl and spin about,
In this place of joy and shout.
For behind every chuckle and grin,
Lies a realm where fun begins.

Tapestry of Untold Stories

In a realm where oddballs reside,
A llama wears socks, and it's quite the ride.
A cat plays chess with a squirrel in glee,
Their champion's crown? A nut from a tree.

A penguin juggles with fish in mid-air,
While a hedgehog recites his best poetry flair.
The sun starts to giggle, the moon does a dance,
In this world of wonder, all creatures advance.

A broomstick races a snail in a race,
Both boost their speed with a loaf of sweet grace.
Even a cactus dons shades, looking cool,
In the strange universe, the odd is the rule.

So come join the circus of whimsy and fun,
Where stories unfold and laughter's the sun.
With each twisted tale, let the joy expand,
In this tapestry woven by humor's own hand.

Bubbles of Transience

A bubblegum bubble floats high in the air,
It winks at the clouds, gives the wind quite a scare.
A mouse in a top hat gives it a chase,
While a dog on a skateboard takes off with great grace.

A bear in a tutu dances with flair,
As bees play the trumpet, without a care.
The flowers giggle, sharing gossip with bees,
In this world of giggles, everyone's at ease.

The bubble pops suddenly, with a plop and a squeak,
The creatures all gasp, "Oh, what a unique!"
Yet, laughter erupts at the sudden twist,
For in this odd bubble, no moment is missed.

So float on these bubbles, let laughter be free,
In the world of the fleeting, let joy just be.
A whirl of delight, like confetti in flight,
Here smiles are as plenty as stars in the night.

Visions in the Breeze

A kite with a grin zooms high with a cheer,
Waving at squirrels, saying, "Come join the pier!"
The breeze carries whispers of stories untold,
As a duck in high heels walks daring and bold.

The clouds dress in stripes as they march in a line,
While frogs sing their songs, sipping sweet lemonade fine.

A turtle in sunglasses just lounges all day,
With dreams made of laughter, come join in the play.

The sun tugs the wind, "Let's dance through the park!"
As a jazz band of crickets plays tunes till it's dark.
Each fluttering leaf joins the whimsical spree,
Creating a symphony bright and carefree.

So sway with the visions that drift on the breeze,
In this playful parade, may your heart find its keys.
With each funny whim, let your spirit be free,
For laughter's the treasure we each hold the key.

Garden of the Forgotten

In a garden where giggles sprout from the ground,
A rabbit in glasses ponders life's sound.
He scribbles in notebooks, on leaves made of gold,
The wisdom of whispers from the stories of old.

The daisies wear hats, and tulips play chess,
While the soil tells tales that never feel less.
A gnome with a party hat waves to a tree,
"Let's hold a parade, come and dance with me!"

The cabbage rolls laughter as it bounces around,
With carrots that juggle, creating pure sound.
In this garden of fancy where whimsies could bloom,
A fortune cookie waits, bringing joy to the room.

So stroll through the path where forgotten blooms sing,
With every step taken, let the merriment cling.
In the laughter of flowers, find solace and cheer,
In this magical garden, there's nothing to fear.

Whispers of the Hourglass

Time ticks and tocks, oh what a sound,
Grains of goofiness all around.
Tickling the toes of a passing breeze,
Wishing for snacks, oh, pass me the cheese!

Upside down clocks at the carnival fair,
Racing with chickens without a care.
Laughter erupts like confetti in air,
Who knew the future could be this rare?

With each grain, a giggle, a snort or two,
Pouring out moments like pancake goo.
Jump in the fun, let the chaos unfold,
In this silly swirl, we're all very bold!

So treasure the ruckus, we dance and we cheer,
For time's just a jester, we've nothing to fear.
With a wink and a nod, we'll frolic and leap,
In the funny abyss, our memories keep.

Mirage of Forgotten Wishes

Floating on wishes like a balloon,
Pineapple pizza? It's never too soon!
Dreaming of llamas in party hats bright,
Bobbing down rivers of fizzy delight.

Wishes take flight on the back of a goose,
Sailing through clouds like a mythical moose.
The unicorn giggles, the dragon just sneers,
As we chase down our dreams with loud, silly cheers.

In this carnival haze, we twirl and we spin,
With marshmallow clouds, let the laughter begin.
Wishes get tangled in cotton candy threads,
While we ride on roller coasters made of bread.

Through laughter and whimsy, our hearts intertwine,
In a whimsical wonderland we'll dine.
Let's gather our wishes and toss them so high,
Where the mirage of fun meets the cotton candy sky.

Echoes Beneath the Stars

Stars wink and smile, playing peek-a-boo,
With socks on our heads, what else could we do?
Chasing the moon on a bicycle swing,
Wonders of nonsense, oh, what joy they bring!

Shooting stars tumble like clowns in a race,
Collecting their giggles all over the place.
A comet whizzes by with a silly face,
Oh to dream wildly in this starry embrace!

With marshmallows soft, we launch into space,
Sipping on moon juice at a lively pace.
Bouncing through echoes, we dance along,
Each twirl a note in our cosmic song.

So let's toast to the light from our fantastical spree,
In the sky's gentle laughter, we forever shall be.
Underneath the stars, with charm we entwine,
The universe hums, and it's all just divine!

Shifting Tides of Reverie

Waves make faces, splashing with glee,
Knitting up dreams by the old banyan tree.
The ocean of giggles, a whimsical ride,
Surfboards are boogers, let's paddle with pride!

Seasick seagulls strut, with hats on their heads,
While jellyfish dance on their spaghetti beds.
With flip-flops for fins, we'll swim in a whirl,
As octopuses giggle and do the twist twirl.

The tides create rainbows of custard and pies,
Whipped cream clouds float under lemony skies.
Splashing in puddles of orange-juice spills,
Sailing through dreams, life's laughter fulfills.

So grab your pie slice, leap into the foam,
With whispers of fun, we will never feel alone.
In the shifting tides where our hearts find their place,
We dance with the sea, in this joyous embrace!

Celestial Pathways

Between the stars, a dance so bright,
My shoes are on, my grip is light.
I tripped on comets, oh what a scene,
Astronauts laughing, oh how they preen.

A space cow floated, munching green cheese,
I asked for a slice, with grace and ease.
She winked at me, then gave a shove,
And off I went, like a rubber glove.

The moon was a beach ball, I tried to kick,
But it flew away, oh what a trick!
Galactic giggles filled the night air,
While planets spun around without a care.

With cosmic pies and glittery wands,
I danced on rings made of rubber bands.
In this wild place where nonsense thrives,
I found laughter in all that survives.

Journey Through Illusions

A rabbit in a tux with a top hat high,
Said, "Follow me, let's fly and try!"
With carrots as tickets, we hopped on clouds,
While giggling fairies danced in crowds.

Mirrors popped up, a funhouse delight,
I waved at my twin, what a curious sight!
We juggled reflections, our heads all askew,
Each glance brought a laugh, oh what a view!

Lost in a maze made of spun candy sticks,
I found a wise owl sharing her tricks.
"Keep your jokes tight, like shoelaces stuck,
And spin like a top, or you're out of luck!"

With giggles galore and tricks up my sleeve,
This whimsical journey, I shall not leave.
In a land where the wildest thoughts play,
I dance with illusions, come what may.

Echoing Footprints

On sandy shores, where footprints play,
I heard them chatter, in funny ballet.
"Who stepped on my toe?" one shouted in fright,
While another replied, "It was just for a bite!"

The waves rolled in, a comical tide,
Tickling toes, in this goofy glide.
With each step forward, the seabirds would squawk,
"Oh no, not that stance, you look like a rock!"

As jellyfish swayed with a wobbly grin,
They joked, "Join our dance, let the fun begin!"
With sandcastles laughing, their turrets askew,
I joined in the madness, as rather a brew.

The tide pulled back, leaving laughter galore,
With echoes of footsteps, forever they'll soar.
As the sun sets low in this silly retreat,
I'll tiptoe through giggles, with joy at my feet.

Serenade of the Abyss

In the deep blue where oddities dwell,
A fish in a bowtie said, "All is swell!"
With bubbles for laughter, they bubbled and spun,
In a circus of wonders, oh what fun!

The crabs played chess, with shells acting stout,
And squids in tuxedos, they all danced about.
"Why do you waltz with that old seaweed?"
One turtle chimed in, "It serves quite the need!"

A treasure chest opened, with giggles inside,
Goldfish juggling coins, what a silly ride!
The octopus winked, his tentacles twirled,
He said, "In this deep sea, let your laughter unfurled!"

So join the parade in the depths of the blue,
Where each little creature shares jokes just for you.
With a serenade echoing all through the dark,
We'll frolic in bubbles, right up to the spark!

Echoes of the Unseen

In the desert of pillows, we dance at noon,
Chasing shadows of laughter, beneath the cartoon.
Footprints of giggles, they vanish too fast,
Like ice cream at sunset, it's gone with a blast.

A mirage of snacks pops up from the sand,
With nachos and dip, oh isn't it grand?
We'd feast with a panda who drinks lemonade,
While planning a party for a sock puppet parade.

Unseen creatures giggle in the heat of the day,
They juggle our worries and send them away.
With a tap of their toes and a wink of an eye,
They leap through our laughter, like clouds in the sky.

So let's skip through the giggles, on clouds made of fluff,

And dance with the daisies, oh isn't that tough?
In this carnival twilight, let's shimmer and gleam,
For what is this life but a fantastic dream?

Oasis of Longing

In a quirky oasis, where cacti wear hats,
And camels break dance with the acrobatic bats.
We sip lemonade sunlight and count every bee,
Who buzzes the chorus of our wild jubilee.

There's a pool made of jelly, a slippery site,
With flamingos on floaties, oh what a sight!
They splash and they tumble, in colors so bright,
Should we join their antics? I think that we might!

A sloth serenades us from high on a tree,
With a ukulele and a penchant for free.
He sings of adventures, both silly and grand,
While a wise old tortoise narrates on the sand.

So let's dawdle a moment in this light-hearted space,
Where wishes float by on a cautious old vase.
We'll dance with the wisps of our fanciful dreams,
Living life in the humor that giggles and beams.

Serenity in Shadows

In the corners of laughter, where whispers ignite,
Shadows chuckle softly, tickling the night.
A cat in a top hat winks from the door,
Offering cookies galore, who could ask for more?

A blanket of twilight wraps snugly around,
With stories of mischief that bounce off the ground.
The moon plays a tune with a sparkle of glee,
As the stars pull their pranks from the cover of tea.

Beneath a great oak, we gather in packs,
With squirrels in tuxedos giving out snacks.
Jokes circle the fire like embers that sing,
As fireflies join in, doing their thing.

Let's giggle in shadows where silliness reigns,
As we toast to the laughter that dances in chains.
Those moments of joy, in the hush of the night,
Find tranquility wrapped in the heart of delight.

Winds of Forgotten Wishes

The breeze whispers secrets of wishes gone by,
With kites made of giggles that dance in the sky.
They twirl and they tumble, chasing after a dream,
Turning chores into games, oh isn't it supreme?

A jester in slippers hops over the fence,
With a sack full of dreams and a truckload of sense.
He juggles our worries and sprinkles in cheer,
Embracing the silly, we cheer and we leer.

The sun tickles toes, like a playful old friend,
Telling jokes about socks that will never quite mend.
With laughter like candies floating on air,
We gather together to share what we dare.

So let's fly on the breezes of whimsical thought,
With tales of adventures that laughter has wrought.
In the fabric of moments, together we twine,
In a tapestry woven with joy, oh so fine.

The Eternal Embrace of Silence

In a world where whispers fly,
Frogs in tuxedos swim on by,
Turtles debating the best pie,
While the stars just laugh and sigh.

Balloons that burst with giggles,
Dance while the crickets wiggle.
A dog in glasses reads a book,
As silence steals another look.

Where shadows play with floppy hats,
And every minute's filled with chats,
A sunbeam tickles, a moonbeam grins,
In the quiet, the laughter begins.

So let us hide from noise, my friend,
Where silence reigns, we shall not end.
For in this quiet, fun shall bloom,
Like candy floss that fills the room.

Underneath the Solstice Sky

Beneath the sky of swirling blue,
A cat in shades plays peek-a-boo.
The grass tickles, giggles rise,
As squirrels sport mini ties.

A duck debates a fancy hat,
While fireflies dance and chat.
In a puddle, a frog tries to glide,
But slips and falls with giddy pride.

Each cloud resembles a silly face,
While sunbeams race in a friendly chase.
Children laugh with ice cream mustaches,
As time floats by in comic flashes.

Oh what a sight, this joyous game,
Where nothing feels the same.
Let's dance beneath this wondrous sky,
And let our hearts take a joyful fly.

Corners of the Infinite Horizon

Along the edge where laughter lives,
Pigs in capes do silly jigs.
Marshmallows float, and cows hold court,
While kangaroos play a wild sport.

Horizons where jokes take flight,
With skits that sparkle in warm sunlight.
A pelican sings a pop tune,
While turtles drum with spoons at noon.

The seagulls dance with flapping wings,
As tiny mice spin out rings.
With every wave, a chuckle flows,
In places where life always glows.

So let us roam these corners round,
Where giggles gather with joyful sound.
A treasure trove of fun awaits,
In laughter locked behind funny gates.

The Mirage Weaver's Lament

In the land where tricks weave smiles,
A rabbit skips in croquet styles.
The mirage giggles, weaves the air,
While cactus spouts a wacky hair.

A dance with shadows, twirl in place,
Where nothing adds up, just pure grace.
The tumbleweed sings a silly song,
As lizards join in, all day long.

A cactus speaks in riddles so bright,
While the sun gives everyone a fright.
In mirage laughter, we chase the day,
Where all the funny thoughts can play.

So here's to mirages that fill the sky,
With twists and turns that make us fly.
In this odd land of whimsical cheer,
Laughter wraps us in its warm veneer.

Celestial Drift

In space, my socks took flight,
They made a dash past the moonlight.
A comet waved, with a squeaky cheer,
I shouted back, 'Hey, what's up, dear?'

The stars giggled, twinkling bright,
Chasing my laundry on this wild night.
Asteroids rolled, in a cosmic race,
While I just stood, with a shocked expression on my face.

Black holes yawned, with a silly grin,
They sucked in laughter, and then threw it in.
Gravity pulled my hair in a swirl,
As I shouted, 'Oh no!' to my cosmic twirl.

But as I floated through this grand sky,
I waved to the planets, and pieced the why.
It's all in fun, this universe scheme,
My laundry's the ticket to a humorous dream.

Mirage of the Heart

In a desert of jellybeans, I found my muse,
Dancing with llamas, in bright rainbow shoes.
My heart did a flip, what a silly sight,
A mirage of love, in the candy moonlight.

Cacti held hands, in the warm desert air,
While squirrels in tutus leaped without a care.
A tumbleweed giggled, rolled past with flair,
And whispered to me, 'Life's a funfair!'

With every step, I slipped on a gum,
The sticky delight made me feel quite glum.
But soon I was twirling, with jellybean glee,
While unicorns cheered, 'Come join us for tea!'

As dusk painted skies with peach and coconut,
I laughed at my heart, oh, what a good nut!
In this crazy realm, where humor does start,
I danced with the llamas, a mirage of the heart.

Ephemeral Starlight

The night was alive with glimmers and smiles,
I rode on a comet, across cosmic miles.
Shooting stars beamed, with wishes so bright,
But all I could think of was pizza tonight!

Galaxies twisted, like a cosmic ballet,
While asteroids bumped, in a goofy display.
I tripped over stardust, and giggled with glee,
'Why can't I float, like a squirrel in the sea?'

Planets played tag, in a spiraling spin,
With Saturn's rings used as a trampoline pin.
Moonlight painted scenes of whimsical cheer,
As I chased a twinkling, rather strange deer.

But fleeting was joy, as dawn's light drew near,
The stars winked goodbye, with a chuckling cheer.
Yet in my heart, this laughter takes flight,
In the echoes of that ephemeral starlight.

Cascades of Memory

Down a river of giggles, I floated so free,
With fish in bow ties, and a crab by me.
They splashed the water, sent ripples of fun,
While I pondered flavors of candy and sun.

A waterfall burst, with sprinkles and cream,
I dove in headfirst, what a wild dream!
A bear wearing glasses, perched on a log,
Said 'Join me for memes!' as I swam through the fog.

In this cascade, memory winks and wobbles,
As squirrels cranked music, launching their gobbles.
Time dripped like honey, so sweet and so slow,
And my heart laughed aloud--where did the years go?

Hopping on turtles, we raced to the shore,
Each splash sounding out with a delightful roar.
In the laughter of moments that bubble and flow,
I danced in the water, letting joy grow.

www.ingramcontent.com/pod-product-compliance
Lightning Source LLC
Chambersburg PA
CBHW072120070526
44585CB00016B/1511